THE TRIPLE A's OF FAITH

DR. R. KEVIN MATTHEWS

"Now the just shall live by faith…"
(Hebrews 10:38a)

GINOSKO MEDIA

The Triple A's of Faith
Published by Ginosko Media

© 2010 by R. Kevin Matthews

Cover design by Donta L. Briggs, Briggs Solutions
www.BriggsSolutions.com

ALL RIGHTS RESERVED. Published in the United States by Ginosko Media. No part of this publication may be reproduced, stored in a retrieval system, or transmitted, in any form or by any means - electronic, mechanical, photocopying, recording, or otherwise - without prior written permission. All inquiries should be addressed to Ginosko Media: info@ginoskomedia.com.

Ginosko Media books may be purchased in bulk at special discounts for sales promotions, fund raising, corporate gifts, or educational purposes. Special editions can also be created to specifications. For details, contact the Sales Department: sales@ginoskomedia.com.

www.ginoskomedia.com

To contact the author forward correspondence to P.O. Box 2368, Shallotte, NC 28459

All Scriptures, unless indicated, are taken from the King James Version Bible.

Library of Congress Cataloging-in-Publication Data is available on file.
ISBN-13: 978-0615980119
ISBN-10: 0615980112

Printed in the United States of America.

DEDICATION

This book is dedicated to my sister Bonnie Kay Matthews, who went on to be with the Lord February 25, 2010. I will be forever grateful for the decisions you made while you were with us. It has been a blessing, and will continue to be a blessing to me, my family, and the ministry to which God has called us to.

I will always remember your generous heart which continued to give unselfishly to me and others, and the impact you had on people that came in contact with you.

You are surely missed in our lives, but your life will be remembered through us by imitating what you did from your heart. You demonstrated love and forgiveness on this journey we're on.

ENDORSEMENTS

Congratulations on a spiritual job well done on your book, Triple A's of Faith. I believe that faith is the key and the way you brought out life experience through the scriptures on faith is outstanding. This is an easy to read book, which means it won't be read halfway through and be tossed on the shelf. It's a must finish to read book. Once again Congratulations.

Apostle, Dr. James W. McGrady Jr.
Jesus Peace Ministries
Fayetteville, NC

I would like to endorse this book by Kevin Matthews. It is a helpful tool of encouragement to those who are receiving the call of Evangelism and/or Pastor Ministry. His expressions of the revelation of the Love of God are coupled with the fruit and gifts of the Spirit, at work by the Holy Ghost. It will spark a hunger in the hearts of those who read it, to devote themselves to the call that God has placed upon their lives for the end-time ministry.

Dr. Frances T. Sullivan (Chancellor)
Brunswick Bible Institute
Shallotte, NC

I have known Kevin Matthews for five years and consider him a friend. He has a heart for ministry and a desire to help others. He also has a gift to write educational materials. I have read the book; Triple A's of Faith, by Kevin Matthews and have found it to be simple, very easy to understand, and presents an inspiring and informative message.

The book is scripturally sound and well written. I would recommend this book to new converts and new ministers as a great asset for their personal libraries.

Pastor, Dr. Bruce Brumfield
East Lumberton Church of God
District Overseer of 21 Churches
Lumberton, NC

ACKNOWLEDGEMENTS

First and foremost I would like to thank my Lord and Savior Jesus Christ for the grace He has shown in my life. I don't know where I would be if it were not for His mercy. I'm surely grateful for my wife Teresa whom God sent my way when I prayed and asked Him for a helpmate in my life. He sent me a best friend.

Thank you also Dr. Dwarka Ramphal for your help with the publication of this book. You stepped in at a time when I was in need. I look forward to working with you more in ministry, for the adding to the Kingdom of God.

Thanks to all my friends and family who have helped in their giving for the publication of this book; and for the prayers and encouragement that came from you I am so thankful. May God return to you favor as well.

God Bless!
R. Kevin Matthews

FOREWARD

There is an old adage that the gospel of Jesus is "simply profound, and profoundly simple." Dr. Matthews has captured this truth in his writing about faith and the believer. He has demonstrated through this work the simplicity of childlike faith and appropriately called this book "The Triple A's of Faith," thereby suggesting that faith is simple.

Yet his insight brings the historical profundity of this approach. He uses a number of everyday analogies to illustrate his journey of faith. Among the everyday analogies he uses to capture the message of faith are those of entering a house or driving a vehicle. Jesus pretty much used similar analogies and parables to capture his teaching on faith. One parable frequently used by Christians to describe faith is the parable of the mustard seed as told by Jesus; even though most American Christians have little concept of the mustard seed or the mustard tree. Dr. Matthews has moved beyond the time specific analogies of faith and draws new analogies to explore the meaning of faith in the new millennium we have entered. Jesus could not have described faith in terms of a motor vehicle, but Kevin can.

The author has explored his faith through his own experience and struggles. It was St. Augustine who noted that God wants us to serve him as humans, not as Gods. So is the life every believer who is tested and tried, and Dr. Matthews is no stranger to the struggles of faith and belief. His vast travels and experiences, coupled with his insight into human nature and his exploration of theology, have enabled him to produce a very readable and inspiring thesis on faith. He has visited and observed many churches and denominations, and he is not easily taken by the public presentation of Christian virtues, but rather delves deeply into the heart of the organization. He looks for Godly faith in addition to other

Christ like qualities, and was often disappointed by what he found to be at the heart of the organization. The periphery of church activities does not fully disguise the heart of worship. Many who have travelled this road will identify with this work.

Dwarka Ramphal Ph.D.
President, New Millennium Ministries
Dunn, NC

TABLE OF CONTENTS

Preface 11

    Chapter 1: What is Faith? 13

    Chapter 2: Fear 25

    Chapter 3: The Triple A's 31

    Chapter 4: Understanding Faith 39

    Chapter 5: The Waiting 43

    Chapter 6: Reality Check 47

    Chapter 7: The War for Your Soul 51

    Chapter 8: Remembering 55

Last Words 59

PREFACE

Even before sitting down to write these words, I realize there are thousands upon thousands of words that have already been written by well-known authors on the subject of faith. However, I can no longer turn a deaf ear to the voice whispering to me, compelling me to share these thoughts with others concerning faith. Although I have preached this material and taught it on many occasions, it never dawned on me, to write a book on The Triple A's of Faith.

This is my first book and I hope these thoughts are just as enlightening for you as they were for me. The Lord taught me these simple principles of faith, using everyday things.

At times it just amazes me how the Lord works. You can be doing something as simple as reading a few lines of scripture during your lunch break and all of a sudden the Lord speaks, opening your spiritual eyes, showing you things you had never seen or understood before.

Now, I thought I had a pretty good understanding of faith. I've read the 11th chapter of Hebrews numerous times, but this day, and days to come, when it became all the more clearer, I realized I was just skimming the surface. Just like Jesus took everyday things by way of parables to teach the disciples, He did the same to teach me.

** It has been some time (many years) since I put to paper the opening words of this book. The Lord continues to show and teach me spiritual mysteries through His word as well as through trial and error on my part. Thank God for the grace and mercy He has shown me as He continues to work in me. May He never cease to do so. Amen

Chapter 1
WHAT IS FAITH?

"So then faith cometh by hearing, and hearing by the word of God."
- Romans 10:17

"Now faith is the substance of things hoped for, the evidence of things not seen."
- Hebrews 11:1

Through faith we understand that the worlds were framed by the word of God, so that things which are seen were not made of things which do appear.
- Hebrews 11:3

"But without faith it is impossible to please him: for he that cometh to God must believe that he is, and that he is a rewarder of them that diligently seek him."
- Hebrews 11:6

"Looking unto Jesus the author and finisher of our faith"
- Hebrews 12:2a

"And beside this, giving all diligence, add to your faith…"
- 2 Peter 1:5a

This last verse leads me to believe that faith is something that you start with and build upon, like the foundation of a house. In order for the house to be stable and secure, it must have a sure foundation. We walk in houses all the time and think nothing about the possibility of the roof caving in on us, or the walls falling down around us. We have a secure feeling that the builders of the houses knew what they were doing. They were careful to follow the laws and codes set up by that state/country so there wouldn't be any problems. They paid special attention to the foundation of the house, especially if it is a grand structure.

Now whether you realize it or not, you have just demonstrated faith. You put your trust and belief in something that you had nothing to do with, and feeling confident that the structure would hold, when you walked in. Do you think a reasonable person would walk in somewhere if he/she thought it would be to his/her harm? Of course not! The laws put in place, will keep the house through years and years, storm after storm, season after season. We do have to realize the houses are manmade, not perfect, and sometimes there will be storms of super strength that will cause damage and in some cases total destruction.

We have a wonderful invention called the automobile which also serves as an appropriate illustration for faith. We simply get into it and turn the key which ignites the motor, bringing it to life, and enabling us to travel to our destination. Again you have just demonstrated faith. Without thinking about it you just did it. You may not have a clue as to how the automobile works as you drive down the road, but still you applied yourself to the truth that it would. Only when the motor does not react as you expect do you realize there's a problem. What the problem is, many of us won't know unless we are skilled in the field.

There are laws that govern the operation of an automobile and when those laws are not in tune with one another, then the automobile is just a hunk of metal. I have some experience with automobiles and know that there are three things needed in order for the motor to come to life. You have to have a spark, which is generated from the spark plugs. You need fuel, like you get at the local gas station. And you need compression which is contents under pressure.

These three acting together are the running engine of a car. One more point though, you can have all three of these and still not have a running engine. The most important component of the three is timing. You have the fuel, which is then compressed inside the chambers of the cylinder, and then at the right time the spark happens that produces the revolution of the engine. The engine's revolutions then turn the transmission, which propels the car to go. Timing, you will find during this faith walk is very important too. God's timing that is. It may not always happen when we want it to, but in God's time it will happen. Timing is very important to God. But, getting back to the automobile, would you get in a car to drive somewhere knowing beforehand that it wasn't going to take you where you wanted to go? Of course not!

Here is another example of how faith works. I work for a company that pays me for the time I spend working for them. I send in a report every two weeks with the hours I have worked and the following week I get a check. They pay me according to the amount agreed to at the time I started working for them. This is the law of the land if you will. They owe me for the time I have given them, to make money for them and to pay me. Let's look at this again. They didn't pay me before I worked, but after I worked. I had to work before I received payment. This again is exercising faith. You put trust in the employer to pay the agreed upon amount for the work you did even before you see any money. Would you go to work for someone if you thought for one second that he/she was not going to pay you for your time? Of course not! It's amazing how much faith we put in people and other things, but do not put the same faith and trust in God, the Creator of all. Let's look at the Word of God concerning God and man.

Moses tells us "God is not a man that he should lie; neither the son of man that he should repent: hath he said, and shall he not do it? Or hath he spoken, and shall he not make it good"? (Numbers 23:19)

Isn't it wonderful to know though that we don't have to work (like we do for man) in order to receive anything from God? All that had to be done has already been done for us. Jesus died on the cross, the debt has been paid, and all he asks of us is to have faith.

> John 16:24 (Jesus speaking) says "Hitherto have ye asked nothing in my name: ask, and ye shall receive, that your joy may be full."

Can it really be that simple? Yes it can! Let's look at the farmer for a minute. He plants a seed in the ground and tends to it until he reaps from the fruit of that plant. Some of us amateur farmers, the ones who have a few tomato plants, or a garden in the back yard, do the same thing. We put in the ground tomato plants, watermelon seeds, okra or corn seeds, then tend to watch and wait for what we've planted until we harvest from that seed.

Do you think the farmer, or us for that matter, would even bother planting a seed, or tilling the ground to get rid of all the weeds, then water it if we felt there was nothing to come from it? I don't think so! So why do we go about in our walk with the Lord, talking with the Lord, having no expectancy for the outcome of our prayers and our relationship with Him? How many of us talk to God with the mindset, "I hope He answers", or even beg and bargain with God in order to receive something. We say we have a relationship with the Lord, but find ourselves answering the questions, "Do you know if you are going to heaven?" with "I hope so." We answer the question "are you saved?" with "I think so." Doubtful and unsure are we of who we are and what we are doing?

Just what is faith? Is it believing? Is it trusting? Is it just saying the words "I believe" that count as faith? Faith is so much more than just believing with the mind or trusting with the heart. It's a surrendered life that experiences times of blessings, times of waiting, times of tribulation, and times of not knowing anything but "God is faithful." Webster dictionary says faith is, "belief and trust in and loyalty to God." Loyalty is commitment to what you believe and trust. It is knowing you are part of a cause greater than yourself, a divine plan.

There was a man name David who one day found himself on the battlefront where Israel was facing the Philistines. This was one of many times Israel and the Philistines faced each other. On this day though, something happened which forever changed the life of David. He went to the battlefront, in obedience to his father's instruction. While there he heard the voice of Goliath shouting out his threats and degrading the God of Israel. Something rose up in David and he began to ask questions.

And David spoke to the men that stood by him, saying, what shall be done to the man that kills this Philistine and takes away the reproach from Israel? For who is this uncircumcised Philistine, that he should defy the armies of the living God?   (1 Samuel 17:26)

His older brother wanted to belittle him for enquiring about the situation. But David's heart was not about to change. God had anointed him for a greater purpose and that purpose was about to show itself. You see he remembered that day that Samuel came and anointed him, that the oil was poured over his head and he recalled the words that Samuel spoke over him. This was not a day that just seemed to happen, but a day that God had prepared. David had been singing about God and who He was during all those times out in the pasture. He was a God of power and strength. He was the same God that gave him power over the lion and bear, to protect the sheep he took care of. God was to be praised and glorified, not mocked and ridiculed. The Spirit of God rose up in David and boldness came upon him, not for show and tell to be noticed, but to stand in the gap and give action to the one he acknowledged and accepted when no one else would.

The same is true for you. There is a purpose for your life. You were not born by chance. You have a calling to the Kingdom of God as everyone else does, to whosoever will. We all have a purpose in the plan of God. Look at this next verse and the question it ask. And David said (to his brother) What have I now done? Is there not a cause? (1Samuel 17:29)

Is there not a cause, a reason, a purpose? I remember this being one of the first sermons I preached that was a turning point in my life. With this one verse God began to open my eyes to the big picture He has with creation and with man. There is a cause (reason, purpose) for my life in service to my Lord.

David turned from his brother to continue what God was doing in him. What his brothers, the king, and all of Israel were fearful in facing, David believed God and was loyal to the call.

I want you to notice that David turned from the negative voice that was speaking to him. That voice was trying to deter him from his calling, his future, and the blessings that comes from walking in faith. Sometimes in spite of family and all that is around us, we have to be obedient to God. Through God using David, the battle was won.

There is a cause (reason, purpose) for you and me as well. Even while you are sitting here reading this, the Spirit of God is talking to you, telling you or reminding you of the call He has for you. He is letting you know the path in life to take, which will bring glory and honor to Him, and blessings to you. We all have a calling in life, a purpose, a reason we were born; fulfilling that call is walking in faith. Look at what God said to Jeremiah.

Before I formed thee in the belly I knew thee; and before thou came forth out of the womb I sanctified thee; and I ordained thee a prophet unto the nations. (Jeremiah 1: 5)

Just as God talked to Jeremiah about his life's calling, so have we been called to a work in the Kingdom of God. I believe there are spiritual callings as well as physical callings to accomplish in this world. There are those called to be doctors, lawyers, teachers, etc. and there are those called into the ministry; Pastors, Teachers, Evangelist, etc. There are also those called to support the ministry. Together we make up the Body of Christ. When we are in the position God wants us to be, that is where God can use us and bless us. Not everybody preaches, not everyone sings, not everyone can play an instrument; however, we all have our purpose.

The Apostle Paul wrote: For as the body is one, and hath many members, and all the members of that one body, being many, are one body: so also is Christ. For by one Spirit are we all baptized into one body, whether we be Jews or Gentiles, whether we be bond or free; and have been all made to drink into one Spirit. For the body is not one member, but many. If the foot shall say, because I am not the hand, I am not of the body; is it therefore not of the body? And if the ear shall say, because I am not the eye, I am not of the body; is it therefore not of the body? If the whole body were an eye, where were the hearing? If the whole were hearing, where were the smelling?

But now hath God set the members every one of them in the body, as it hath pleased him. And if they were all one member, where were the body? But now are they many members, yet but one body. And the eye cannot say unto the hand, I have no need of thee: nor again the head to the feet, I have no need of you.

Nay, much more those members of the body, which seem to be more feeble, are necessary: And those members of the body, which we think to be less honourable, upon these we bestow more abundant honour; and our uncomely parts have more abundant comeliness. For our comely parts have no need: but God hath tempered the body together, having given more abundant honour to that part which lacked: That there should be no schism in the body; but that the members should have the same care one for another. And whether one member suffers, all the members suffer with it; or one member be honoured, all the members rejoice with it. (1 Cor. 12:12-19)

One of the first experiences I remember having with God concerning faith, happened soon after I was saved. I was working at a dime store in town and payday was coming. I wanted to buy a new pair of boots to wear to church. I think the only thing I had to wear at the time was tennis shoes. I wanted to get something to wear that was dressier, something like what others wore. Well, after going over in my mind the hours I had worked, multiplied by my rate of pay, on the surface it didn't seem like I could buy those boots. Going over it again and again in my mind, it just didn't seem possible. I don't remember what all I had to do with my pay. I was only fifteen and did not have a lot of bills. At the time I did help my mother with some of the household bills, or groceries. We were not well off. Anyway, there was a moment when I was thinking about those boots while putting together a bike in the back of the store. Something happened to me that I still remember today. This overwhelming calm came over me and this voice spoke inside of me. "You can get the boots." Even in my baby stage of mind, I recognized it was the Lord speaking to me. Although I had gone over it several times in my mind, I knew I could get those boots. I also remember later though while wearing the boots at church, one of the other teens saying something about them. Evidently I was out of style but, I had the boots and that's all that mattered. Isn't that the way the devil is? When God does something in your life, he tries to bring negativity around to spoil the blessings of God.

The same thing happen when I was first saved. I didn't know anything about God. I wasn't raised in a Christian home. Even after the Lord saved me there was doubt that I was even saved. I went for a few days with this question of doubt, but then the Pastor talked with me letting me know it was the devil putting thoughts of doubt into my head. Doubt wasn't there before I went to the altar. The devil will always try to bring doubt and confusion to tear down what God is doing in our life. He is and always will be a liar!

I think this is a great opportunity to say to you, without the Spirit of God working in your life, faith cannot be. Jesus is the author and finisher of our faith. The Comforter (Paraclete), whom Jesus talked of sending back after He ascended to Heaven, is God (the Holy Ghost) working in the world to bring people to Himself. What Jesus did while on the earth, the Comforter continues to do in the life of the believer. And everything He does in the life of believers is to bring glory to God, to help the believer in the purpose God has for him in the Kingdom of God. It is not to bring attention to him/her for the individual's glory or gain. Man's love thinks of himself first, God's love thinks of others first. God forbid I should reduce the word of God, which is my spiritual nourishment, or use whatever gifts and talents God has blessed me with and try to use it for profit or gain. Not by man's might or by man's power, but by my Spirit says the Lord. Jesus said, "No man hath ascended up to heaven, but he that came down from heaven" (John 3:13)

This leads me to believe it all starts in heaven. I wasn't looking for Jesus when I became aware of Him. He was always there, but I didn't know it. Then the day came when I was made aware of Him. He caught my attention. When I accepted Him as my savior, He began a work in me. I will never get to the point where I will not need the Holy Spirit to be there, working in me concerning my life with God.

People need to understand you can do all kinds of things from jumping, running, shouting, praising, preaching, teaching, and singing unto the Lord, but He does not accept you and you alone. It's the Jesus in you that started in heaven, which makes you alive, that He accepts. The Holy Spirit in you returns to heaven in the form of jumping, or shouting, and is accepted by God the Father.

While sitting here writing this, something has come to me about the presence of God. You know in the Old Testament, the children of Israel knew when the presence of God was with them. God provided the Ark of the Covenant to be the visible sign of His presence. When they went to war and the ark was in the camp, there was no fear to go out against the enemy. They knew God had their back so to speak, but when the ark wasn't in the camp, it was a different story. We have the ark with us today as well. The Spirit of God that dwells in us is our Ark, glory to God! We have the assurance of God's presence by His spirit dwelling in us; talking to us, teaching us His way and giving His power to us. In this power we are more than conquers through Him that loved us. (Rom. 8: 37) What a mighty God we serve!

There is a man I know, a business owner whom I briefly worked for. He told me something one day I still remember. In all the years this man has been in business, he told me he has found there are two types of workers. One is hungry, has bills to pay, comes to work early and leaves late. Then after a couple of paydays he starts to slowly shift into someone different. He is not as hungry as before. His bills are paid. He comes in late and leaves early. There is a spiritual lesson here. God is there all the time; the good times, and the bad times. Do we give Him the same treatment? Are we fat and happy, having need of nothing these days? Or do we really just hunger and thirst for God only when there are problems? God help us.

The other worker, he said, comes in the first day and does a pretty good job, looking around to get a scope on the job becoming familiar with the business and such. The next day he comes in and tries to tell you how to run your own business, the business you've had for longer than a day. Could there be a spiritual lesson here as well? I'll leave that with you and God.

God has recently shown me something. My life is about letting Him be Lord of my life. A lot of us know Jesus as the Savior of our life, as I did, but not Lord. He has shown me I need to trust in Him completely. I thought that is what I had been doing. Knowing God has called my wife and me into the ministry; it has been my agenda to visit other churches when not at our church. While visiting these churches, it was part of my thoughts that the preacher there, or someone, would be a connection to help further our ministry. Now this is not a bad thing, cause God can and will put people in your path that will be beneficial to you. The difference God has shown me though is that when He is not leading me, I might be able to connect with others who may only bring limited opportunities. But when God is leading and making the connection, the opportunities are unlimited. God knows where I need to be and where I need to go to fulfill the call upon my life. When He is leading, there are blessings and the things He has spoken to me about will come to past. When He is not leading, then I'll be in store for a great education. Education cost you know! It has been said that having a Mentor will help you not make too many mistakes.

Chapter 2
FEAR

Fear is the opposite of faith. Faith compels you to keep pressing forward. Fear keeps you from moving on. The devil uses fear and tries to detour you from believing that God is able and willing to keep you, and then bless you in the way He's leading. Fear says, "No you can't" while faith says, "yes you can". Fear makes a situation or circumstance look bigger than God. Faith tells you that God is bigger than anything this world throws at us, and fear just brings doubt and confusion. However, when we keep our minds on God, He will keep us in perfect peace (Isaiah 26:3). We are His children and He is our Father. "Either your faith will change your circumstances, or your circumstances will change your faith." There is:

- Fear of dying if sickness has attached itself to you.
- Fear of not achieving goals that are before you.
- Fear of not being able to overcome that which is trying to bring/keep you in bondage.

The norm in this world is to have something to help you maintain your sanity while dealing with all the stuff that we come into contact with. Now, don't get me wrong, I am all for using medicine when it is needed to help, but as I have done in the past, when I was running from God, I took to drinking, drugs, and even companionship- something that would help ease the pain and emptiness I felt in my soul. What I found out and now know is that it was all a trick of the devil to keep me from surrendering to God. The more he could keep my mind on the temporary fix, I was never able to see the eternal liberty found only in Jesus.

One night the disciples were in a boat going to the other side of the sea as instructed by Jesus. Looking out they saw someone walking on the water. Afraid and anxious they wondered who, what and how? They realized it must be Jesus:

> "Peter answered him and said, "Lord, if it be thou, bid me come unto thee on the water."
>
> - Matthew 14:28

This is a remarkable scene. You see Peter was no stranger to the water. He was a fisherman whom Jesus called one day to follow Him. The "water" was his territory being a professional fisherman. He had been on the water, in the water, and under the water if you will. No doubt the water had troubled Peter once or twice before.

I was in the Navy and at different times stationed on two ships. I've been to sea many times- to the Caribbean, across the Atlantic Ocean and back. I have been swimming in water so deep you could not fathom the bottom. I've seen the water calm just like bath water, and I've seen the same water become what looks like mountains at sea. The ship would go down in the swell and all you could see was water on both sides. Then it would go up on top of a wave and you could clearly see the roughness of the water all around us. When it was time to go to sleep you had to be tied in your bunk. If you were on watch, you were tied to the rail of the ship so as not to be washed overboard. A rope was tied from one end of the ship to the other enabling you to walk forward and aft. We held onto the rope helping us to walk to the chow hall and back. Once in the chow hall you were challenged to eat while holding onto your tray and glass at the same time. Believe me, at times all I wanted was five minutes of stillness on shore. The constant motion worked on my sanity.

Peter had been there and done that so to speak. He was not a stranger to the water. Now, here he is in the boat, a familiar place, seeing the miraculous; Jesus walking on water, without hesitation Peter asked Jesus to bid him to come unto Him. As the saying goes, be careful what you ask for. Before you proceed out into the depths you must know it is something you believe with all your heart God is leading you to do. Peter, at times being the impulsive one, was not blinded by the situation. He believed in Jesus, and was convinced that what Jesus did, he (Peter) could do also. "Bid me come unto thee on the water." Peter said. The most important part of this story is not that Peter did walk on water, but what happened when he went from what I call "single sight" to multiple sights. When we keep our eye on Jesus and the call He has placed within us, we need to remember to keep our eye on Jesus. Don't worry so much about what is or is not happening around us. In other words don't let it dominate your mind and cause it to make decisions you might not need to make.

> "The light of the body is the eye: if therefore thine eye be single, thy whole body shall be full of light."
> - Matthew 6:22

In single sight we are focused on one thing, although we can still see things that are not clear in our peripheral vision. They are not clear because we are not focused on them. In multiple sights we are affected by everything that is happening around us whether they are important or not.

In order to get to Jesus, Jesus had to be the main focus for Peter, but he started to have multiple sights and began to sink. When we feel the Lord is calling us to something, I believe He gives us single sight. Keep the main thing the main thing. If we will continue on the path it will grow until we have the full picture. If we begin to listen to what others say our focus becomes multiple sighted and the vision becomes distorted. If I had listened to some of the people in my life I would not be where I am today. You know those negative voices that say:

- I don't believe you were called to preach.
- I don't know if you can really get anyone to start a church or not.
- I don't think you were called to be a Pastor.
- Doesn't sound like a joyful noise to me when you're singing.
- How can you teach or preach when you can't even read?
- You've got too much of a past to do anything for God.
- Nobody cares about your philosophy of life.

And the list goes on and on. On the other hand, there are some people I should have listened to. They could have helped me to see better than I did at the time. Again, education cost!

Peter walked on the water while his eyes were on Jesus. His focus was to get to Jesus. Remember Peter asked, "bid me to come." He did not hide in the boat, or secure himself in the boat. Peter was not an amateur on the water. He saw the water and heard the water; he heard the wind and no doubt felt it on his person. Still, he desired to do as Jesus did. Peter stepped out of the boat and began to walk on the water towards Jesus. Just before he got to Jesus, Peter developed multiple sightedness. Focusing on the elements around him, he became afraid and began to sink. In fear, he cried out, "Lord save me." Immediately Jesus stretched forth His hand and caught him. Jesus said unto him,

> "Oh ye of little faith, wherefore didst thou doubt?"
> - Matthew 14:31

If Peter had kept his eye on Jesus, he would have walked to Jesus then back to the boat with Jesus. Faith is surrendering to what is not common to the natural eye; doing the impossible when all you can see is what's possible.

The devil's sole intention is to keep you from fulfilling your purpose in the Kingdom of God. The Spirit of God will lead and guide you. He will help you overcome all the trickery he uses that brings doubt and confusion to stop you.

Trust in the Lord with all thine heart; and lean not unto thine own understanding. In all thy ways acknowledge him, and he shall direct thy paths. (Proverbs 3:5, 6)

Chapter 3
THE TRIPLE A'S

It was in the year of 2000 when I was reading the Bible during my lunch hour at work that I came across the passage in 2 Peter 1:5, which says, "That giving all diligence add to your faith…"

The word "add" suddenly stood out and exploded in my mind as the Holy Spirit began to teach me about faith. "Add to your faith". In order to add to something, "something" has to be there first. According to this verse it's "faith" that has to be there. I viewed this idea of faith like a foundation; as in the construction of a house or any building. You must first have a solid foundation before anything else can be done. While pondering the thought of faith as a foundation, there were three words that came to me suddenly. They were acknowledge, accept, and action.

In all my years as a Christian listening to other ministers, I've never really heard anyone that I recall preach about the definition of faith in its deepest sense. Is it believing? Is it trusting? Sure, it's believing! Sure, it's trusting! However, faith is much deeper. It is not just a mind thing; it's a heart thing as well, a total life giving commitment to something. Faith is something you totally surrender to, believe in and trust in. It is like the house you walk into or the car you get into to drive down the road. Faith is working for the company or boss you trust to give you a paycheck when its payday. That's what faith is. It's not just saying, "I believe" or "I trust"; it goes much further than that. It's walking the walk, not just talking the talk.

The three words that come to me are what I refer to as "the Triple

A's of Faith". In thinking along those lines that day, I started thinking about the foundation. My first thought about the foundation, of course, is houses and buildings which I covered in Chapter 1, as well as the farmer who plants in order to receive a harvest. There is an action, on my part, necessary to demonstrate my faith. James the Apostle wrote, "For as the body without the spirit is dead, so is faith without works is dead also". (James 2:26)

Of course we know that we cannot work for our salvation, for we are saved by grace, not works, but the works are part of being saved. I go to church, read my Bible, pray, witness to others, not to be saved, but because I am saved.

Remembering my experiences when I was first saved, these "triple A's of faith" were working in me whether I was aware of it at the time or not. The same is true for you. Whether you were listening to a radio program, watching television, or just listening to somebody witnessing about the love of Jesus, you knew you needed what they were talking about. There was an emptiness inside that could only be filled by this Jesus you were hearing about. First we have to acknowledge, or we become aware of the need, or the emptiness in our life, and that Jesus is the answer to fill that void. Webster defines acknowledge as: to admit the truth or existence of something, to recognize the rights, authority, or status of something.

What I was hearing about caught my attention and somehow I knew it was truth. There was a God and He made it possible for me to be a part of Him. He was creator and sustainer of all that is in existence. Without Him I was lost and with Him all things were possible. God is the power.

Let us say that someone is trying to get your attention to talk to you. Only when you acknowledge that individual will you be in a position to receive what the person is trying to say. I tell my wife to make sure I'm looking at her and she has my full attention when she is going to tell me something I need to remember or is important. If I'm doing something else at the time, she might not have my full attention. Then later when she asks me about what she said, I will know what she is talking about.

On the job or at school when someone is communicating to you, you don't need to be distracted by something else. They need to have your focus on them, because it could make a big difference when comes to being accountable.

The next step, if you will, is acceptance. According to Webster, acceptance means to receive with consent or approval, or to receive as true. I had to accept or "surrender" to what I had just acknowledged. What I realized with my understanding, I had to become a part of that acknowledgement. I needed to acknowledge, and accept this Jesus I heard about.

Now during this time of acceptance, we all struggle within ourselves whether or not to respond to this call. I'll cover more why this is in another chapter. It's different with everyone, what we go through in our minds during this life changing event. It's a war being fought over your soul, but you really don't understand this warfare. All you know is you are faced with a decision. Your heart is racing, and there seems to be an overwhelming conviction. One part of you is saying to run; another part wishes it'll be over soon. Then there is that "still small voice" simply saying, surrender. This is the decision. Once we have accepted what we have acknowledged, then we come to the action. Webster defines action as the working of one thing on another so as to produce a change, the doing of something usually in stages or with the possibility of continuation. Don't you just love that definition? "The working of one thing on another."

The action is the proof that I am saved and I'm not the same way I use to be. The natural body is the same, but there has been a transformation of the mind. It no longer thinks as it did before. My transformation happened instantly and continues to work in me. When that occurs, we, who are saved, know of the weight lifted off our shoulders. We know a transformation is exactly what happened. The sin and ignorance that held us captive, weighing us down has been removed. We become a new person with new thoughts and a new outlook on life.

One day Jesus was on His way to bring healing to someone and in the mist of the crowd a woman touched Him resulting in her being healed of an issue of blood. The Bible says this woman had battled with this disease for twelve years (Matthew 9). She had spent all the money she had at the doctors, yet instead of getting better she grew worse. She no doubt heard of Jesus doing marvelous works in and around the area. The blind saw, the lame walked, and water was turned into wine. She had acknowledged this is where I could receive my healing. He is the one with the power. Next, she had to accept (surrender) to whatever it took to get to Him. She needed to get to Him, somehow, some way, to let Him know of her condition. But the crowd surrounded Him, making it difficult to reach Him. She could have thought who am I to deserve such healing? Surely not anyone of importance. Actually, in her condition she wasn't even supposed to have contact with people. But she knew she had to reach Jesus somehow. Then it came to her, if she could just touch His clothes that could be enough. How many of us have been to this point when we knew what we must do to get the victory, and all that is left to do, is just to do it. I believe at this point the devil throws all he can at us. It's all right to come to the knowledge of victory, but victory is not victory until we surrender to and act upon it. Until we push through the crowd, with all that is in us, reaching until we can make contact or touch God in order to get the victory, can we receive our miracle.

There was a phrase once used often in church, "Pray until you pray through". This woman pushed through the crowd until she touched the clothes of Jesus and instantly she was made whole. By her actions she was demonstrating her faith. Oh yes! It may seem hard at the start and the devil may be fighting you, but victory can be yours!

The Bible tells the story of a paralytic man lying on a cot and bound by his condition (Matthew 2). Thankfully he had four friends who wanted to see him free and knew (acknowledged) where they could bring him to be healed. Oh, to have friends that are willing to go the extra mile for you and with you, so you could have the victory. God help us to be able to see beyond our own four walls. Anyway, these friends (accepted and acted) carried this man who knows how far, to get to Jesus. Jesus is the answer for all your issues, inabilities, and ignorance. Now when they got to Jesus, there was a crowd. We don't know how long it took them to get there, or how long they would have to wait in line in order to get this man next to Jesus. Sometimes we have to forget about manners and protocol. There are desperate times when we need an answer from God. Desperate times need desperate actions.

No doubt these friends were knowledgeable of the carpentry work of those days. Either one or more of them said, "If we can just get to the side of the house and up on the roof, we can get in." I believe there were others there that had all kinds of thoughts concerning maneuvering around the crowd, but the Bible doesn't say specifically. The Bible does say the circumstances didn't stop these friends. They pressed through and got to Jesus. As a result of their actions, their friend was healed.

One day as Jesus was entering into Capernaum, a centurion came to Him on behalf of a servant, at home sick of the palsy. Jesus was going to the man's house to touch him and heal him, but the centurion said, "Lord I am not worthy that you should come under my roof, but speak the word only and my servant shall be healed." The Bible says, Jesus "marveled" and said, "I have not found so great faith in Israel." (Matthew 8)

Lord, help us to know you are everywhere. We are not limited to the preacher laying hands on us in order to receive. Just speaking the word in faith brings results.

Another illustration is the story of Bartimaeus. Here was a blind man that heard Jesus was passing by. He too acknowledged that Jesus had the power to heal him, and he surrendered to what it took for that to happen.

He must get Jesus' attention as He passed by. He cried out, "Have mercy on me." And just as it happens so many times when we get an unction to step out in faith, there are those that want to shut us up. Don't cause a scene or interrupt the service as it's going along. Don't bother the man of God; there are protocols that have to be followed.

Bartimaeus didn't care about protocols or disrupting an agenda. He needed healing and this was his moment to get it. Even though they told him to be quiet, he cried the louder, "Jesus, have mercy on me." When Jesus came to him and asked him what he wanted, he said, "to receive my sight." Jesus replied, "Go thy way; thy faith hath made thee whole." (Mark 10)

There was another blind man that Jesus came across who had been blind from birth (John 9). Jesus spat on the ground and made clay, then anointed the eyes of the blind man. There are times maybe when we think, "just a touch from the hand of the Master", and all will be fine. But here Jesus touched the man and then gave an instruction to follow through in order to get his healing. How many of us have not followed through or even heard an instruction from God when we have prayed?

My Pastor, who has gone on to be with the Lord, used to tell me in my earlier walk with the Lord that I was lazy. And what he meant by that was I did not press on with whatever was going on at the time, until victory came. I did not have the patience to wait it out or keep working it out. Oh, how many times was I just at the winner's line and didn't receive at that time because I became frustrated or just quit.

There was another one that comes to mind in the Old Testament that might not have received his healing were it not for a reality check by his servants. His name was Naaman.

Naaman was Captain of the host of the king of Syria. A great man and honorable, but the bible says he was a leper (2 Kings 5). When he heard of a man in Israel that could heal him, the king sent money and clothes along with a letter to the king of Israel. Elisha heard about Naaman and called for him to come to him. When he came to the house of Elisha, Elisha sent out a messenger and gave a simple instruction, "go dip seven times in the river Jordan." Naaman was upset because everything he thought might happen didn't. Does this sound familiar in anyway?

Simple faith, like the centurion had for his servant, "just speak the word only, and my servant shall be healed."

Chapter 4
UNDERSTANDING FAITH

How does this happen, being "born again"?

The Bible says man is a spirit. We also have a body and mind. The body is the house our soul (intellect, emotions) occupies. The spirit is like the current running through the house. It gives energy, motivates, encourages, and activates just like the electric current in your house. There is a saying, "a person's spirit is low or high," and it reflects their mood. This means we all have a will which enables us to choose what we want to be and depending on circumstances, it will reflect in our attitude towards life. Every day we are faced with decisions. The ones we choose determine the outcome, good or bad. In other words there are consequences to every decision. (Galatians 6:7, 8)

When we make the decision to surrender to the Spirit of God, we do just that. It's no longer you or I determining or controlling our existence, but the God we have surrendered to and continue to surrender to. It's not just being obedient one time or even once in a while, it's a continual life experience. When we surrender to God it's a lifestyle till the end, for we no longer live for our self, but for the glory of God. Paul said," I die daily" (1 Cor. 15:31). What our mind wants us to do because of the carnality in us, has got to surrender to the mind of Christ so that we might glorify Him and not ourselves. Jesus came to the earth and illustrated the will of God by His obedience all the way to the cross. What He did while on the earth was an example to us today. The Bible says, we receive a measure of faith, but Jesus had no measure. He had all the power and performed such in the healings that took place and control of the elements on the earth. His life was not about popularity. He had an attitude of servitude.

I remember the testimony of one of my professors concerning his conversion. He tells of one night while in the Navy, he became aware of sin in his life and the need to repent and accept the Lord. He said he remembered kneeling down beside his bunk, asking the Lord to forgive him and come into his life. From that day forward he was different. He knew he was saved. Romans 10:9 if thou shall confess with thy mouth, the Lord Jesus, and shall believe in your heart that God hath raised him from the dead, thou shall be saved.

He remembers it because it was a life-changing event. That's what we refer to as being "born again". Just as we celebrate our birthdays, we remember the day that the Lord saved us. After completing his military tour he went on to college. In time, he went from being a Youth Pastor at one church, to Senior Pastor at another church. He has also taught at several colleges and recently earned a Doctorate of Divinity Degree at the local college. This is what happens when we surrender to the call of God. We all have hopes and dreams in life we want to accomplish. What is yours? Does it include the Lord?

Recently the Lord brought this thought to my attention. When we are born, the Spirit of God breathes life into this body. Everything living, man and animal, has this breath of life in them. I believe man, when he is born is given from God the desire/need to praise Him in order to fulfill the call in their lives. There are also things that will not bring praises to God, which is part of the carnal man, selfishness. What we exercise ourselves in, to become strong in, will determine who we are. The gifts of God, when we walk in them, bring praise to God, not ourselves. As we continue to exercise ourselves in these gifts they become stronger in us. If we are not glorifying God in our life, then we are serving the devil. Our lives show our strong points. Profoundly, those who are constantly changing what they are exercising themselves in, will not grow at all. One offsets the other and at the end the rewards are minimal. James says,

> "A double-minded man is unstable in all his ways. Let not him think he shall receive anything of the Lord."
>
> - James 1:8

Faith is of God, and as Jesus came and died unselfishly for our redemption, so our lives are not about us. It is all about Him. When we ask for things, is it selfishly for ourselves or is it for the benefit of others? When we put others first, God will look out for us. It's not about how good we sing, preach and teach, or any other abilities. It's always about Him. Two ways you can know if someone is following God or promoting self. If what they are doing is not for the saving of a soul or the benefit of edifying the body of Christ, something is amiss.

Chapter 5
THE WAITING

The waiting period we have to endure is probably the hardest of all. In times of contentions, you are doing something whether you like it or not. In times of trouble, you are dealing with something. Your mind is focused on the problem at hand pondering how to make it a positive experience instead of defeat.

In waiting, you want to reach out to others seeking advice and comfort. You call asking for prayer, which they can and will do, but this is your waiting time and right now prayer is not the answer. You listen to music, read your Bible, trying to find anything to do besides just sitting and waiting. You fight your feelings so you can continue to work your job, take care of the house, and be the husband or wife you need to be. Life is going on, but for you it is just a waiting period.

You watch Christian television looking for and hoping for a word to sustain you during this time of waiting. You sow seeds of faith hoping God will hurry in what he is preparing for you. You can just see the after effect when God has blessed you and promoted you to your next level in the kingdom of God as a business owner or executive of a business, Pastor of a church or planting a new church, Music Minister instead of just being a member of the music team. You feel like crying out to God at times to relieve the pressure that seems to be building up in your mind. GOD WHERE ARE YOU???

Years ago I was visiting a church service and the pastor said something that night which has stuck with me. He said the Lord taught him something that day about "waiting." He was visiting one of his members in the hospital. When he walked by the surgery waiting area, the Lord spoke to him and said, "They have to wait." He realized the people there could not do anything, but what they were doing. WAITING! They could not help the surgeon, could not assist the nurses, or be in the same room with them. All they could do was wait. It's hard at times not knowing what the next moment will bring, good or bad.

> Faith is the substance of things hoped for, the evidence of things not seen.
>
> - Hebrews 11:1

In times like this God is doing His work. God is faithful even when we're not. It may not seem like God is in control, but He is. The only thing we can do is keep ourselves in control. What we do during this time will have an effect on the coming days. You see being faithful to God is the most important thing. Knowing what He has told you He would do no matter how long ago, He will do it. If we will listen and be faithful to the cause, He will bring it to pass. His word is sure and He is not a man that will back out of His promises. We trusted Him for salvation, we trust Him for eternal life, and we can trust Him in the little things as well as the big. HE IS FAITHFUL! HALLELUJAH!!!

Let faith have its perfect work in us until it is completed. The faith Jesus started in us He will perform until the end. Part of the action in this book is you just have to know that sometimes there is no action on our part. Know, even in the waiting period there is an unseen action. Waiting can be a very powerful time. (Phil 4:6) Be careful for nothing; but in everything by prayer and supplication with thanksgiving let your requests be made known unto God. (Romans 12:7a) Let us wait on our ministering: I was in church service one night and the preacher made this statement, "Faith that cannot be tested cannot be trusted." Abraham, the Father of faith, came to a time of testing none of us will probably ever face. After the blessing of a son in his old age, Abraham was asked to sacrifice him to the Lord.

I do a lot of reading and one day I read this on a pamphlet. These are not the exact words, but close. "There can never be any public demonstration of Jesus in your life, until there has been private imputation of Jesus in your life." Think about it!

Chapter 6
REALITY CHECK

While writing this book I gained a new insight in looking at "the Triple A's of Faith". It takes all three of the "triple a's of faith" in order for it to be complete. You see, you can acknowledge something, but not ever accept it. Therefore, there will be no action. You can have action, but it's no good without acknowledging or accepting. You can accept something, but not agree to acknowledge it and the action will be negative.

To illustrate this; let us say you get a job where the boss is like a CEO or someone on that level. However when you meet him, you don't like him, or he turns you off by something he said or did. My favorite example is that he just reeks of his position, and knowingly, or unknowingly, lets everyone know it. You see, you can acknowledge his position; he signs your paycheck and the buck stops there so to speak, however, you have no respect for this person. There's no insight you can gain from this person, nor can he have an influence in your life. There is only a contract, you do your job and he pays you for it. No real relationship.

One day a man who had many riches came to Jesus and said: Master what good thing shall I do, that I may have eternal life? (Matthew 19:16) The man said he had kept the commandments from his youth up. Then Jesus said, "If thou will be perfect, go and sell all that thou hast and give to the poor, and thou shall have treasure in heaven: and come and follow me." (Matthew 19:21) The Bible says he went away sad because he had many riches. He acknowledged Jesus' power but never surrendered to it. The riches were more important. Jesus never had an impact on this man and we never read about him again.

Now, let's look at Acceptance. Reflecting on this word, I realized to accept something is to surrender to it. You don't argue with it, you don't try to modify it, you don't try to analyze it. You simply recognize the power and surrender to it. To illustrate this, we can see surrendering to something only when we are forced to, like law enforcement. You can't over take them or out run them. There is no choice. Refusing to acknowledge the power your actions are negative and detrimental.

Finally, let's examine action. You can perform an action, but not have any power because you never surrendered. Years ago I was talking with a pastor about what I refer to as the liberality of church people. I'm not really an "out there" kind of person. Actually I'm quite reserved if you know what mean. I realize there are people that live life real loud and out there. I'm not saying that's wrong; it's just not me. Anyway, he said something to me I remember. He said sometimes there is just a "spirit of the air" that moves in the church. You know, "feel good, goose bump" kind of thing. I realized there are dangers in both areas. On the one hand, if you are too reserved, you might quench the Spirit of God by not responding to it. On the other, if you are too free, if you will, you might see more into something than there really is.

There can be action, but if there is no acknowledgment of power and surrendering to it, the action is wrong or even in vain. In the Bible this is illustrated in the action of the Pharisees. Jesus said to do what they say but not as they do. There were others that tried to buy the power when they saw it being displayed. Being religious is different than being saved and delivered. Also, there were the sons of Sceva who tried to demonstrate the power they saw in Paul. The end result was the devils jump on them and tore them to pieces. They wanted what others had, but did not acknowledge or accept the power.

This is a dangerous state to be in. One verse which has bothered me as long as I can remember is where Jesus says, "I do not know you" (Luke 13) speaking of those that will come to Him saying we have done this in your name and that in your name. Jesus would not have made this statement if it were not a fact. There is grace and mercy, but I recognize there are also limits even with God.

The term Christian these days has taken on a totally different persona. The word comes off the tongue so slippery. Saying it has just become a byword, like a coat that you take off and on depending on the weather; a word to drop when dealing in a certain crowd in order to gain something. It has lost the power it once had. Originally it described a group of people that stood for and preached, with signs following. They continued what Jesus had begun, to proclaim the good news and the kingdom of God.

I have mentioned in times past of having "radical faith." This radical view does not lead you to bombing abortion clinics. Love does not intentionally do harm to others. Radical faith is taking an unmovable stand for the cause of Christ. It is grasping the cross and what it stands for, and to commit to a life which does not seek glamour or wealth. Faith is much bigger than that. People have given their lives because of what they believed to be truth, choosing against all odds to live that truth. Not to bring up bad memories, but there are those who strap bombs to themselves, giving their lives to do harm for a cause. They trained a long time to hijack planes for what they believe to be the truth, willing to give their lives for it.

What have we reduced Christianity to today? Is God pleased with what He sees? At what point do we change?

Chapter 7
THE WAR FOR YOUR SOUL

How did all this start? Why do I struggle in life between doing the right thing and the wrong? What is the right thing? What is my purpose in life? Where is my life headed? Questions, questions, there seem to be endless questions. I know there are those more educated, with a greater understanding who can better explain what the gist of it all is, but here is my finiteness trying to explain the infinite.

In reading the word of God, there were several passages that gave me some insight and allowed God to help me understand what it's all about. Now I know this may be somewhat different from what others have concluded, but it has helped me tremendously. You see, I was the person who could only live for today. I had no plan for the future, i.e. marriage, career. This had a lot to do with my upbringing. Some of us spend a lifetime trying to overcome things experienced during our growing years. It's getting worse because children are being brought up without any awareness of God at all. No church, no prayer. Often their exposure is drugs, divorce, abuse, sports, and money. We're raised with motives which are not entirely detrimental to our lives, but do not teach us the need for the Savior of our souls.

Ezekiel 28 and Isaiah 14, I believe give insight to what happened in the heavens before the foundation of the earth we know today. We read in Ezekiel of one called Lucifer who is a created being like all angels. Lucifer was the music minister in the heavens conducting a joyful noise, praising God the creator. Now before anything was created, I believe God, infinite and all power knew of the rebellion to come through Lucifer who wanted to be a god vs. just a worshipper of God. This is exactly what we do today when we do not surrender to the call of God. We want to be in control of our own lives. However, what we choose to do determines our outcome. Even if we state we are not going to choose between serving God or the devil, when we reject God, we are serving the devil. You might think because you're a good person and there is no trouble in life; being happy the majority of the time, that you are in good standing with God. The truth is the devil has no need to mess with someone when they are not serving God. He knows if you have not given your life to Christ, your life belongs to him. We are all born in sin. Sin is the devils domain.

I will do this, and I will do that, to follow his own will was Lucifer choice. He chose not to acknowledge the one that created him. Can the thing which is created say to Him that created it, I will do whatever I want? The idea of self will was the birth of sin. God knowing this "blot" would bring imperfection to creation (for God only creates perfection). He created a way to redeem creation, doing away with the "blot". I refer to this as the Covenant of Redemption.

I have only heard this covenant referred to two other times in my life. Once, while I was attending school and the other time was recently on television. Now, this is something that the Lord open up to me even before the Triple A's of Faith. So God (Father, Son, and Holy Ghost) before creating anything put forth a plan of redemption, in that 'the Christ' would be the atonement for sin and redeem man back unto God. So this war, the war for your soul, takes place between God and the devil over all of God's creation. The devil persuaded a third of the angels to go with him at the time of his rebellion. He wants to turn all creation against God, demanding all to serve him. Thank God he was defeated at the cross.

He could never defeat God being "created" of God. The devil tries all he can to defeat your life. He brings confusion and chaos into people's lives trying everything he can to persuade you to reject God as he did. His destiny has already been sealed and hell awaits him. Because of the hatred he has toward God, he wants to cause problems in everyone's life. He still wants to be worshipped as god and when we reject the Lord, we are doing his will.

Jesus came being obedient unto death for the sins of the world, to reconcile that which was lost through Adam. Through the word of God we get an understanding of our purpose and the plan God has for our lives. We have the Holy Spirit to help us in fulfilling that purpose.

Chapter 8
REMEMBERING

How did all this start? Why do I struggle in life between doing the right thing and the wrong? What is the right thing? Jude writes: To exhort that we should earnestly contend for the faith, which was once delivered unto the saints (Jude 3).

To me, this is "putting rubber to the road" kind of faith. It's getting involved where we can make a difference, putting action where we believe that God can and will bring about a change. Acknowledging He is God, accepting the purpose and plan He has for your life, and allowing God to use you in a demonstrated way for His glory; for the salvation of a love one, the healing of a friend, or the opening of a door where we can't see one.

I believe even the Old Testament saints are included in this sentence. We have a great historical record of men and women who trusted God in child birth, when going out to fight wars for the righteousness of God, when appointing kings, and being delivered from the enemy of their souls as well as from slavery. Hebrews 11 covers a lot of the honor roll of the believer who gave their life for faith. The old hymn says,

"Jesus, Jesus how I trust thee,
How I proved Him o'er and o'er.
Jesus, Jesus precious Jesus.
Oh for grace to trust Him more."

Proverbs 3:5, 6 trust in the Lord with all your heart and lean not on your own understanding, in all thy ways acknowledge Him, and He will direct your paths.

Bruce Winston wrote a book titled "Be a leader for God's sake". In his book he takes the beatitudes and gives them a whole new meaning in reference to leadership in the work place. The first of these is, "Blessed is he that is poor in spirit for theirs is the kingdom of heaven." (Matthew 3:5)

He writes to be "poor in spirit" is to realize we never know it all and always have a "teachable spirit" about us. Jesus had faith without measure, but we are always using just a measure of faith. We read in Mark's gospel of a son who was possessed with a demon spirit which caused his father much grief. His son would rant and rave, foaming at the month trying to bite people, causing mental and physical pain. The spirit would throw the son through fire and water trying to kill him. The father heard, no doubt, about the healing going on in Jesus' ministry and brought him to the disciples to be healed and delivered from this pain. The disciples could not cast out this demon. Then Jesus came on the scene and said to the father, "If thou canst believe, all things are possible to him that believeth." (Mark 9: 23)

Faith is believing and to him that believes all things are possible. And straightway the father of the child cried out, and said with tears, Lord, I believe; help thou mine unbelief. (Mark 9:24) Help my unbelief. That's the place we need to stay if you will. Knowing what God has done in our life, what God is doing in our life, and what God is going to do in our life. We have not and will not attain the highest until we are no more in this body.

I'd like to say right here everyone is important in this world. We never get to a point where we don't have need of someone. As preachers and teachers of the word, we are called out and separated for the work of

God, but never are we above the people of God. Everyone the Lord has brought your way is needed. Every one of them has talents and abilities that will complement your ministry, and not one is more important than another. I often pray God will remind me where He brought me from and help me in treating everyone He has bless to come under my ministry with the same respect. Even Jesus was faced with those who wanted to make Him more than what He came to be. He said He knew what was in man, but He came to fulfill the Father's will.

In Luke 17:6 the Apostles ask Jesus to "increase our faith." This is where Jesus says, "If ye had faith as a grain of mustard seed, ye might say unto this sycamore tree, be thou plucked up by the root, and be thou planted in the sea; and it should obey you."

Jesus uses the illustration of a servant in obedience to his call, to show the glory belongs to Him. It's the Lord that calls, qualifies, and opens the doors for you to go through, to accomplish His desires. When we are in tune with the calling, His desires become our desires. No matter how many books we write, how many degrees we attain, or how big a church we Pastor, we have only been obedient to the faith God granted us to complete. There are rewards in being obedient to God and the calling, but the greatest is when we pass over to eternity.

LAST WORDS

Have you accepted the will of the Father? Are you doing what is needed in your life that will be for His glory and your benefit? Or are you being defeated by something that has happened or what someone has said to you? I come across people all the time who have quit going to church or given up in some way because of something that happened in their life. I've been there myself many times. I've had my hole which I crawled into so I couldn't be hurt or affected by church people. When it all comes down to it, I'm the one who has to stand before God and give an account. He has reached out to me many times and reminded me He couldn't use me or bless me in my hole. That is what His desire is, to bless you and use you for His glory. There is a position only you can fill. It's up to you to surrender and trust God. God's love is unconditional, but His blessings are conditional. Conditional as in obedience to accepting His son, Jesus Christ, and allowing the Holy Spirit to work the word in us and through us.

There are three areas in my life God has shown me to be in obedience. Where I live, where I work, and where I attend church. He will show you where you need to be and what you need to do as well.

"Yea, a man may say, Thou hast faith, and I have works: show me thy faith without thy works, and I will show thee my faith by my works."

- James 2:18

Paul, in his writings, spoke of faith in these churches saying:

- I thank my God through Jesus Christ for you all, that your faith is spoken of throughout the whole world. - Romans 1:8
- That your faith should not stand in the wisdom of men, but in the power of God. - 1 Cor. 2:5
- Watch ye, stand fast in the faith, quit you like men, be strong. 1 Cor. 16:13
- …for by faith ye stand. - 2 Cor. 1:24b
- But they had heard only, that he (Paul) which persecuted us in times past now preaches the faith which once he destroyed. - Gal. 1:23
- Wherefore I also, after I heard of your faith in the Lord Jesus, and love unto all the saints, Cease not to give thanks for you, making mention of you in my prayers; - Eph 1:15-16
- There is one body, and one Spirit, even as ye are called in one hope of your calling; One Lord, one faith, one baptism, One God and Father of all, who is above all, and through all, and in you all. - Eph 4:4-6
- Yea, and if I be offered upon the sacrifice and service of your faith, I joy, and rejoice with you all. - Phil 2:17
- Remembering without ceasing your work of faith, and labour of love, and patience of hope in our Lord Jesus Christ, in the sight of God and our Father; - 1 Thess. 1:3
- For from you sounded out the word of the Lord not only in Macedonia and Achaia, but also in every place your faith to God-ward is spread abroad; so that we need not to speak anything. - 1 Thess. 1:8
- We are bound to thank God always for you, brethren, as it is meet, because that your faith grows exceedingly, and the charity of every one of you all toward each other abounds; - 2 Thess. 1:3
- When I call to remembrance the unfeigned faith that is in thee, which dwelt first in thy grandmother Lois, and thy mother Eunice; and I

am persuaded that in thee also. - 2 Tim. 1:5
- Hearing of thy love and faith, which thou hast toward the Lord Jesus, and toward all saints; - Philemon 1:5
- That the communication of thy faith may become effectual by the acknowledging of every good thing which is in you in Christ Jesus. - Philemon 1:6
- For unto us was the gospel preached, as well as unto them: but the word preached did not profit them, not being mixed with faith in them that heard it. - Hebrews 4:2
- Let us draw near with a true heart in full assurance of faith, having our hearts sprinkled from an evil conscience, and our bodies washed with pure water. Let us hold fast the profession of our faith without wavering; Hebrews - 10:22-23
- Now the just shall live by faith... - Heb 10:38a

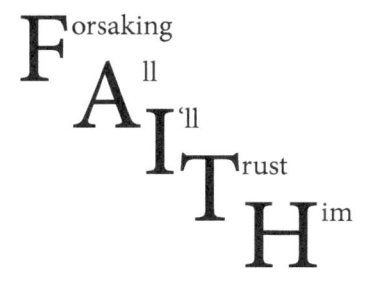

Forsaking
All
I'll
Trust
Him

Solo Fide!

ABOUT THE AUTHOR

Kevin Matthews, originally from St. Pauls, NC, is married to the former Teresa Core McLamb from Erwin, NC. They presently reside in Shallotte, NC where they moved in 2008 to begin a work for the Lord.

Kevin attended Heritage Bible College in Dunn, NC majoring in Religious Education with a concentration in Pastoral Studies. In 2010, he finished the requirements needed to receive a Master's and Doctor's in Evangelism and Pastoral Ministry through Brunswick Bible Institute located in Shallotte.

Over a period of 25 years, Kevin has worked in various churches assisting in the musical area as guitarist, drummer and singer, as well as preaching and teaching. Along with his wife Teresa, they Pastored River of Life Church in Lumberton, NC in 2005.

In March of 2008, Kevin and Teresa founded Foundation of Faith Ministries, based upon the Triple A's of Faith book. Their hope is to have an impact on the local community, preaching the Gospel of Jesus Christ and teaching the principles found in these writings; also, to teach the principles of "purpose, position, and prosperity". That we all have a purpose in the Kingdom of God, a place or position to fulfill that purpose, and then God can and will prosper you, in helping you fulfill that purpose, in that position, equipping you in order so to minister to others.

Kevin and Teresa have a vision of building a "Christian Retreat" on the water where they live, that would be beneficial to many for retreats, seminars, and time away from everyday life, to draw closer to the

Lord. They are available for ministry. You may contact them for further information.

Foundation of Faith Ministries

P.O. Box 2368

Shallotte, NC 28459

910-755-7614

E-mail:

revmata3@yahoo.com